Redefine Your Reality: Shifting Mindsets for Breakthrough Success

Cyprian Ahuchaogu

GLIM PUBLISHING LTD

Published by GLIM Publishing Ltd, United kingdom (London)

Edited by: GLIM PUBLISHING

Cover design: GLIM PUBLISHING

Image sources: GLIM PUBLISHING LTD

Printed on unbleached acid-free paper.

Subscribe to our newsletter. Simply write to glimpublishing@gmail.com or visit our website https://glimpublishing.co.uk/

Contents

Dedication

To the seekers of truth and architects of change,
This book is dedicated to all who dare to dream of a better self and a better world. To those who believe in the power of transformation and the potential that lies within each heart and mind.
For the courageous souls who have embarked on the journey of self-discovery, for the tireless warriors battling their inner demons, for the silent heroes whose acts of kindness light up the darkest corners, and for the faithful who walk in trust and hope – this is for you.
To my family, for their unwavering support and love, and to my mentors and friends, whose wisdom and encouragement have been my guiding stars.
And above all, to the grace of God, which sustains, guides, and enriches our journey every step of the way.
May this book light a path for your journey and be a companion in your moments of doubt and triumph.
With gratitude and hope,
Cyprian Ahuchaogu

Foreword

Foreword

As I pondered the themes of transformation, faith, and personal growth that form the heart of "Redefine Your Reality: Shifting Mindsets for Breakthrough Success," I was immediately struck by the profound simplicity and depth that Cyprian Ahuchaogu brings to these complex subjects.

In a world that often feels chaotic and unpredictable, this book emerges as a beacon of clarity and wisdom. It doesn't just speak to the mind; it resonates with the soul. Cyprian has woven together timeless biblical principles with modern psychological insights, creating a tapestry that is both beautiful and practical.

This book is a journey – one that invites you to explore the depths of your own being, to question, to reflect, and ultimately, to transform. It is for anyone who has ever felt stuck, anyone who has ever yearned for change but didn't know where to start. It's for those who have faced adversity and those who have celebrated triumph. In short, it is a book for all of us.

Cyprian's approach is not prescriptive; it is exploratory. He doesn't give you the answers; he guides you to discover them. Each chapter is meticulously crafted, leading you gently but firmly towards a deeper understanding of yourself and your place in the world.

What is particularly striking is the way Cyprian integrates Christian faith into every aspect of personal development. He reminds us that spiritual growth and personal success are not mutually exclusive but are, in fact, deeply interconnected. This book is a testament to the power of faith in shaping a successful and fulfilling life.

As you turn these pages, you will find yourself challenged and comforted, provoked and pacified. You will be asked to look inward, to confront your fears, and to embrace your potential. You will be encouraged to see the world not as it is, but as it could be – through the lens of faith, hope, and love.

In closing, I urge you to read this book with an open heart and a curious mind. Let it be your guide as you seek to redefine your reality and embark on a path of breakthrough success.

Warm regards,

Petra Omenaka

Preface

Preface

In the quiet moments of reflection that often precede the birth of a book, I found myself contemplating the profound journey of personal transformation. This book, "Redefine Your Reality: Shifting Mindsets for Breakthrough Success," is the culmination of that contemplation, a labor of love born from both personal experience and a deep-seated desire to share the insights I've gathered along my journey.

The decision to write this book stemmed from a simple yet powerful realization: we are all architects of our own reality. Our thoughts, beliefs, and actions shape the world we live in, and by altering these, we can transform our lives. However, this transformation is not merely about achieving success in the conventional sense; it is about finding a deeper, more meaningful connection with ourselves, with others, and with God.

Throughout these pages, you will find a blend of Christian and biblical principles, psychological insights, and practical advice. This fusion is intentional. I firmly believe that true transformation and breakthrough success are holistic, involving not just the mind but also the heart and spirit.

Each chapter of this book addresses a different aspect of personal growth and development, from overcoming fear and cultivating resilience to building strong relationships and leaving a lasting legacy. The journey is not always easy, but it is undoubtedly rewarding. My hope is that this book will serve as a guide, a source of comfort, and a catalyst for change in your life.

As you embark on this journey of transformation, remember that it is a deeply personal and unique experience. There is no one-size-fits-all approach. I encourage you to approach each chapter with an open mind and heart, ready to explore, question, and discover.

Thank you for choosing to embark on this journey with me. May the pages that follow not only inform you but also inspire and empower you to redefine your reality and achieve breakthrough success in every area of your life.

In faith and service,

Cyprian Ahuchaogu

Chapter One

Introduction

Redefine Your Reality: Shifting Mindsets for Breakthrough Success" embarks on a transformative journey, inviting you to reshape your understanding of success, leadership, and personal growth through the lens of Christian principles and psychological insights. This book is not just a guide; it's a catalyst for change, challenging you to reevaluate your perceptions and beliefs, empowering you to achieve breakthrough success in various facets of life.

The journey begins with "Embracing a New Vision: The Power of Perspective." This foundational chapter urges you to step back and view your life from a fresh perspective. It lays the groundwork for understanding how our thoughts and beliefs shape our reality, and how altering these can lead to profound changes in our lives. The chapter draws on biblical wisdom and psychological principles to illustrate how a shift in perspective can unlock new possibilities and opportunities.

"The Mindset of Overcomers: Thriving in Adversity" delves into the resilience and strength that come from a mindset geared towards overcoming challenges. It teaches you how to find strength in your faith and inner resources during tough times, turning obstacles into stepping stones for growth.

"Transforming Thoughts: From Negative to Empowering" takes you through practical steps to rewire your thinking patterns. It highlights the importance of positive affirmations, prayer, and mindfulness in reshaping your thought processes. This chapter blends scriptural wisdom with cognitive behavioral techniques to demonstrate how changing your thoughts can change your life.

"The Faith Factor: Trusting Beyond Sight" emphasizes the role of faith in navigating life's uncertainties. It explores the concept of faith not as a passive acceptance but as an active, dynamic force that shapes our approach to life's challenges.

"The Leadership Mind: Guiding Others Through Change" shifts focus to the impact of our mindset on those around us. It discusses the qualities of servant leadership and how leading by example can inspire and uplift others. This chapter draws from the life of Jesus and contemporary leadership theories to present a model of leadership rooted in humility and service.

"Building Resilient Relationships: Keys to Harmonious Living" emphasizes the importance of strong, healthy relationships in our lives. It provides insights into developing and maintaining relationships that are resilient in the face of life's ups and downs, using principles from scripture and relationship psychology.

"Prayerful Reflections: Aligning Your Will with the Divine" encourages a deep, contemplative approach to prayer. It explores how prayer can be a powerful tool for self-reflection, guidance, and aligning our desires with God's will.

Each subsequent chapter builds on these themes, weaving together scriptural references, psychological research, and practical advice. From navigating life's challenges to cultivating gratitude and leaving a lasting legacy, this book covers a spectrum of topics relevant to anyone seeking a deeper, more meaningful, and successful life.

"Redefine Your Reality: Shifting Mindsets for Breakthrough Success" is more than a book; it's a journey towards a transformed life, grounded in faith and enriched by practical wisdom. Whether you're looking to deepen your spiritual walk, enhance your relationships, or achieve new heights in your personal and professional life, this book offers the tools and insights you need to make it happen

Chapter Two

Embracing a New Vision: The Power of Perspective

*I*ntroduction

As we embark on the journey of "Redefine Your Reality: Shifting Mindsets for Breakthrough Success," the first step is to embrace a new vision. This chapter is about understanding the power of perspective and how it shapes our reality. Perspective is the lens through which we view the world, interpret our experiences, and make sense of our existence. It's a foundational element in shaping our thoughts, actions, and ultimately, our life's trajectory.

The Concept of Perspective

The concept of perspective is not just about seeing things differently; it's about understanding that how we see things can fundamentally alter our experience of life. Just as a painter chooses a vantage point to create a piece of art, we too choose, consciously or unconsciously, the perspective from which we view our lives. This perspective can be limiting or liberating, depending on how we frame it.

Shifting Your Perspective

Shifting your perspective begins with acknowledging that you have the power to choose your viewpoint. This shift involves moving from a passive to an active stance in life. It's about moving from 'things happen to me' to 'I can influence what happens.' This shift is empowering and liberating.

Perspective and Faith

In a Christian context, perspective is closely tied to faith. Faith is the assurance of things hoped for, the conviction of things not seen (Hebrews 11:1). It's about seeing beyond the immediate, tangible reality to a deeper, spiritual truth. Shifting your perspective in line with your faith means seeing your life not just as a series of random events but as part of a divine plan, guided by a loving God.

The Role of Mindfulness

Mindfulness plays a crucial role in shaping our perspective. It's about being present in the moment and aware of our thoughts and feelings without judgment. Mindfulness helps us step back and observe our habitual thought patterns, many of which shape our perspective unconsciously. By becoming more mindful, we can start to choose our perspective more consciously.

Changing the Narrative

Our life narrative is the story we tell ourselves about who we are, what we've been through, and where we're going. This narrative is powerful, and it shapes our perspective. By changing this narrative from a negative to a positive one, from a story of victimhood to one of victory, we can transform our perspective.

Practical Steps to Shift Perspective

1. **Gratitude Practice:** Start and end your day by listing things

you're grateful for. This practice shifts your focus from what's missing or wrong to what's present and right.

2. **Reframing Challenges:** When faced with challenges, ask yourself what you can learn from them and how they might be helping you to grow.

3. **Seeking Different Viewpoints:** Actively seek out and consider perspectives different from your own. This expands your worldview and fosters empathy.

4. **Mindful Meditation:** Incorporate daily meditation focused on presence and awareness. This helps in recognizing and altering automatic thought patterns.

Conclusion

Embracing a new vision by shifting your perspective is the first step toward redefining your reality. It requires mindfulness, faith, and the willingness to change your narrative. As you start to see the world differently, you'll notice a change in how you respond to life's challenges and opportunities. This chapter is your starting point for a journey of transformation, where a new perspective opens the door to a life of breakthrough success.

Chapter Three

The Mindset of Overcomers: Thriving in Adversity

Introduction

Welcome to Chapter 2 of "Redefine Your Reality: Shifting Mindsets for Breakthrough Success." In this chapter, we delve into the mindset of overcomers, focusing on how to thrive in the midst of adversity. Life is replete with challenges, but it is our response to these challenges that defines our journey and shapes our success. This chapter explores how to cultivate a mindset that not only withstands adversity but also uses it as a catalyst for growth and transformation.

Understanding Adversity

Adversity comes in many forms: personal loss, professional setbacks, health challenges, or spiritual trials. While these experiences can be daunting, they also present opportunities for deep personal growth. Understanding adversity involves recognizing its potential to strengthen and refine us.

The Biblical Perspective on Adversity

Scripture provides numerous examples of individuals who faced immense challenges and emerged stronger. Consider Joseph, who endured betrayal and imprisonment before rising to a position of power in Egypt. His story teaches us about resilience, faith, and the redemptive power of God working through our struggles. Similarly, the book of James encourages believers to consider it pure joy when facing trials, as these test our faith and produce perseverance (James 1:2-4).

Shifting Your Mindset in the Face of Challenges

To thrive in adversity, we must shift our mindset from one of victimhood to one of victory. This shift involves:

1. **Recognizing the Role of Adversity:** Understanding that challenges are not just obstacles, but opportunities to grow and learn.

2. **Maintaining a Positive Outlook:** Keeping faith and hope alive even in the darkest times.

3. **Learning from Failures:** Viewing failures as stepping stones rather than stumbling blocks.

The Power of Resilience

Resilience is the ability to bounce back from setbacks and adapt to challenging circumstances. Cultivating resilience involves:

1. **Building a Strong Support System:** Surrounding yourself with people who uplift and encourage you.

2. **Staying Connected to Your Faith:** Drawing strength and

comfort from your spiritual practices and beliefs.

3. **Developing Emotional Intelligence:** Understanding and managing your emotions in healthy ways.

Practical Strategies for Overcoming Adversity

1. **Problem-Solving Skills:** Approach problems with a mindset of finding solutions rather than dwelling on the difficulties.

2. **Self-Care:** Prioritize your physical, emotional, and spiritual well-being.

3. **Setting Realistic Goals:** Break down overwhelming challenges into manageable steps.

Conclusion

The mindset of overcomers is characterized by resilience, positivity, and a deep-rooted faith that transcends circumstances. By embracing this mindset, we can transform our experiences of adversity into powerful moments of growth and success. This chapter lays the foundation for thriving in the face of life's challenges, encouraging you to see adversity not as a barrier but as a pathway to greater strength and achievement.

Chapter Four

Transforming Thoughts: From Negative to Empowering

Introduction

In Chapter 3 of "Redefine Your Reality: Shifting Mindsets for Breakthrough Success," we delve into the transformation of thoughts. Our thoughts have immense power over our emotions, actions, and ultimately our lives. This chapter explores the journey from negative, self-defeating thoughts to a mindset filled with empowering and positive affirmations, aligning with Christian principles and psychological insights for a holistic approach to mental transformation.

Understanding the Power of Thoughts

Our thoughts are the seeds from which our reality grows. Negative thoughts can create a reality of fear, doubt, and limitation, while positive, empowering thoughts can cultivate a reality of hope, confidence, and possibility. The Bible speaks to the power of thoughts and their influence on our lives (Proverbs 23:7). Understanding this power is the first step towards transforming our thought patterns.

Identifying Negative Thought Patterns

Many of us have ingrained patterns of negative thinking that have developed over years. These might include self-doubt, fear of failure, or feelings of unworthiness. Identifying these patterns is crucial in beginning the process of transformation. This involves mindfulness and self-reflection, recognizing when and why these negative thoughts arise.

The Role of Scripture in Transforming Thoughts

Scripture provides a rich source of positive affirmations and truths that can counteract negative thoughts. Verses like Philippians 4:13, "I can do all things through Christ who strengthens me," offer powerful reminders of our identity and capability in God. Integrating these truths into our daily thought life can profoundly reshape our mindset.

Practical Steps to Transform Thoughts

1. **Mindful Awareness:** Regularly practice mindfulness to become aware of your thoughts and the patterns they form.

2. **Positive Affirmations:** Replace negative thoughts with positive affirmations, both scriptural and personal.

3. **Cognitive Behavioral Techniques:** Use techniques such as reframing or challenging negative thoughts to alter your thought patterns.

4. **Prayer and Meditation:** Engage in regular prayer and meditation, focusing on the truths and promises of God.

Overcoming Mental Barriers

Transforming thoughts also involves overcoming mental barriers such as fear, anxiety, and limiting beliefs. This requires a combination of faith, resilience, and practical psychological strategies. By leaning into your faith and using tools like visualization and affirmations, you can start to dismantle these barriers.

Creating a New Narrative

As your thoughts begin to transform, so does the narrative of your life. You move from a story defined by limitations and fear to one marked by potential and hope. This new narrative shapes not only how you view yourself but also how you interact with the world around you.

Conclusion

The journey from negative to empowering thoughts is a pivotal aspect of redefining your reality. It requires consistent effort and a deep commitment to mental and spiritual growth. As you engage in this transformative process, you'll find that your thoughts become a powerful force for positive change in your life, aligning your mindset with God's plan and unlocking your true potential for breakthrough success.

Chapter Five

The Faith Factor: Trusting Beyond Sight

*I*ntroduction

Chapter 4 of "Redefine Your Reality: Shifting Mindsets for Breakthrough Success" dives into the essence of faith and its transformative power in our lives. Entitled "The Faith Factor: Trusting Beyond Sight," this chapter explores how faith, especially in the Christian context, acts as a powerful force in shaping our realities, guiding our decisions, and providing a foundation for overcoming life's challenges.

Understanding Faith

Faith, in its simplest form, is complete trust or confidence in someone or something. In a Christian perspective, it's the assurance in God's promises, His character, and His plan for our lives, even when circumstances seem contrary. Hebrews 11:1 defines faith as "the substance of things hoped for, the evidence of things not seen." This chapter unpacks this definition, exploring how faith transcends mere belief and becomes a tangible force in our lives.

Faith and Perspective

Faith has a profound impact on our perspective. It allows us to see beyond the immediate challenges and uncertainties, focusing instead on the bigger picture of God's plan. This shift in perspective is not about denying reality but about framing it within a larger, divine context. We explore how faith empowers us to face adversity with hope and confidence.

The Role of Faith in Decision-Making

Faith also plays a crucial role in decision-making. It guides us in times of uncertainty, providing a moral and ethical compass grounded in Christian principles. The chapter delves into biblical examples, such as the wisdom of Solomon and the faith-driven decisions of the Apostles, to illustrate how faith informs choices and leads to divinely guided outcomes.

Strengthening Your Faith

Strengthening faith is a journey, not a destination. This chapter provides practical steps to cultivate a stronger faith, including:

1. **Regular Prayer and Meditation:** Developing a deeper relationship with God through consistent communication.

2. **Scriptural Study:** Engaging with the Bible to understand the promises and teachings that form the foundation of Christian faith.

3. **Community Involvement:** Participating in a faith community for support, learning, and growth.

4. **Faith in Action:** Applying faith in practical ways in daily life to reinforce trust in God's guidance.

Faith in the Face of Doubt

Doubt is a natural part of the faith journey. This chapter addresses how to navigate doubts and uncertainties, viewing them not as failures of faith but as opportunities for growth and deeper understanding. We explore the balance between faith and reason, and how to maintain faith in the midst of a skeptical world.

Conclusion

"The Faith Factor: Trusting Beyond Sight" emphasizes that faith is not a passive acceptance but an active, dynamic force in our lives. It's about trusting beyond what we can see, leaning on God's promises, and letting this trust transform our reality. This chapter encourages readers to embrace faith as a key component of their journey towards breakthrough success, offering a blend of spiritual insight and practical guidance for living a faith-filled life.

Chapter Six

The Leadership Mind: Guiding Others Through Change

Introduction

In Chapter 5 of "Redefine Your Reality: Shifting Mindsets for Breakthrough Success," we turn our focus to leadership. Titled "The Leadership Mind: Guiding Others Through Change," this chapter explores the intersection of personal transformation and leadership. It examines how developing a leadership mindset, grounded in Christian principles, can not only transform us but also empower us to inspire and guide others through periods of change.

Understanding Leadership

Leadership is often misunderstood as a position of authority or power. However, true leadership is about influence, guidance, and service. It's about guiding others through change and challenges while maintaining a vision of success. We explore the Biblical perspective of leadership, highlighting figures like Moses and David, who led with humility, courage, and reliance on God.

The Qualities of a Leadership Mind

A leadership mind is characterized by several key qualities:

1. **Vision:** The ability to see beyond the present situation and envision a better future.

2. **Empathy:** Understanding and relating to the feelings and perspectives of others.

3. **Integrity:** Consistently aligning actions with values and principles.

4. **Resilience:** The capacity to face challenges and bounce back stronger.

Servant Leadership

The concept of servant leadership, exemplified by Jesus Christ, is central to this chapter. It emphasizes leading by serving others, putting the needs of others above one's own, and leading by example. We explore how servant leadership not only transforms those who are led but also the leaders themselves.

Leading Through Change

Change is a constant in life and a critical aspect of leadership. This chapter provides insights into how effective leaders navigate change, not just by adapting themselves but also by helping others adapt. This includes fostering a culture of openness, encouraging innovation, and managing the emotional and practical aspects of change.

Practical Strategies for Developing a Leadership Mind

1. **Self-Reflection:** Regularly reflecting on your actions, motivations, and their impact on others.

2. **Continuous Learning:** Committing to personal and professional development.

3. **Mentoring and Coaching:** Both seeking mentorship and mentoring others as a way of developing leadership skills.

4. **Prayer and Spiritual Growth:** Deepening your spiritual life to guide your leadership journey.

Conclusion

"The Leadership Mind: Guiding Others Through Change" emphasizes that leadership is about more than just leading; it's about transforming. It's about embracing the qualities of vision, empathy, integrity, and resilience, and guiding others to do the same. This chapter encourages readers to adopt a leadership mindset that is rooted in Christian values, empowering them to be effective leaders in all areas of their lives, from personal relationships to professional endeavors.

Chapter Seven

Building Resilient Relationships: Keys to Harmonious Living

*I*ntroduction

In Chapter 6 of "Redefine Your Reality: Shifting Mindsets for Breakthrough Success," we focus on the art of building and maintaining resilient relationships. Titled "Building Resilient Relationships: Keys to Harmonious Living," this chapter delves into the principles and practices that foster strong, healthy, and enduring relationships, rooted in Christian values and psychological insights.

The Importance of Relationships

Relationships are the cornerstone of a fulfilling life. They provide support, joy, and meaning. However, relationships also face challenges and require resilience to thrive. This chapter explores the significance of relationships in our lives and the impact they have on our overall well-being and success.

Biblical Principles for Relationships

The Bible offers profound wisdom on relationships. Principles such as love, forgiveness, patience, and kindness are foundational for resilient relationships. We examine these principles through scriptural examples and teachings, illustrating their relevance and application in modern relationships.

The Role of Communication

Effective communication is vital in building and maintaining resilient relationships. This includes active listening, expressing thoughts and feelings honestly and respectfully, and understanding non-verbal cues. The chapter provides practical tips for improving communication skills and overcoming common communication barriers.

Managing Conflicts

Conflict is an inevitable part of relationships, but it doesn't have to be destructive. This chapter discusses strategies for managing conflicts constructively, including the importance of empathy, negotiation skills, and seeking win-win solutions. It also highlights the need for forgiveness and reconciliation, drawing on Christian teachings about grace and mercy.

Building Emotional Resilience

Emotional resilience is key to maintaining strong relationships. It involves the ability to manage one's emotions, cope with stress, and bounce back from setbacks. The chapter offers guidance on developing emotional resilience, including self-awareness, self-care, and stress management techniques.

Creating a Supportive Community

Building resilient relationships extends beyond personal connections to creating a supportive community. This involves nurturing a network of friends, family, and peers who provide encouragement, advice, and a sense of belonging. The chapter discusses the role of church and community groups in fostering this sense of connectedness.

Conclusion

"Building Resilient Relationships: Keys to Harmonious Living" underscores the importance of strong relationships in our journey to success and fulfillment. By applying Biblical principles, improving communication, managing conflicts constructively, and building emotional resilience, we can create and maintain relationships that not only endure but thrive. This chapter encourages readers to invest in their relationships, seeing them as integral to a life of breakthrough success.

Chapter Eight

Prayerful Reflections: Aligning Your Will with the Divine

Introduction

In Chapter 7 of "Redefine Your Reality: Shifting Mindsets for Breakthrough Success," we delve into the profound practice of prayer and its role in aligning our will with the divine. Titled "Prayerful Reflections: Aligning Your Will with the Divine," this chapter explores how prayer can be a transformative tool in our personal development journey, offering insights into how it connects us with God, provides guidance, and aligns our desires and actions with His plans.

Understanding the Power of Prayer

Prayer is more than a ritual or a religious obligation; it is a way of communicating with God, expressing our thoughts, desires, and concerns. It is a channel through which we seek guidance, gain insight, and find peace. This chapter emphasizes the importance of prayer in Christian life and how it can profoundly impact our mindset and actions.

Aligning Our Will with God's

One of the most challenging yet rewarding aspects of prayer is learning to align our will with God's. This requires humility, trust, and the willingness to surrender our plans and desires. We explore biblical examples, such as Jesus in the Garden of Gethsemane, to illustrate this concept of surrender and alignment with God's will.

The Role of Meditation and Contemplation

In addition to prayer, meditation and contemplation are crucial for deepening our relationship with God. These practices involve quieting our minds, focusing on spiritual truths, and allowing God's word to penetrate and shape our thoughts and perspectives. This chapter provides guidance on incorporating these practices into daily life.

Overcoming Barriers to Effective Prayer

Many people struggle with prayer, facing barriers such as doubt, distraction, or a sense of unworthiness. This chapter addresses these challenges, offering practical advice on how to overcome them and cultivate a more meaningful prayer life.

Practical Tips for Prayerful Reflection

1. **Setting Aside Regular Prayer Time:** Establishing a routine for prayer and sticking to it.

2. **Journaling:** Writing down prayers, thoughts, and reflections to enhance focus and clarity.

3. **Using Scripture in Prayer:** Incorporating biblical verses and passages into prayer to enrich understanding and connection.

4. **Community Prayer:** Engaging in collective prayer with others to experience the power of communal worship and support.

Conclusion

"Prayerful Reflections: Aligning Your Will with the Divine" emphasizes the transformative power of prayer in our journey toward success and fulfillment. By fostering a deeper prayer life, we open ourselves to divine guidance, align our desires with God's will, and find the strength to navigate life's challenges. This chapter encourages readers to embrace prayer as a vital tool in their personal and spiritual growth.

Chapter Nine

Navigating Life's Challenges: Strategies for Endurance

*I*ntroduction

Chapter 8 of "Redefine Your Reality: Shifting Mindsets for Breakthrough Success" addresses a crucial aspect of personal and spiritual growth: navigating life's challenges. Titled "Navigating Life's Challenges: Strategies for Endurance," this chapter explores practical and spiritual strategies to endure and thrive amidst life's inevitable trials and tribulations, drawing on Christian principles and psychological resilience techniques.

Understanding Life's Challenges

Life's challenges come in various forms: personal loss, health issues, career obstacles, or spiritual trials. These experiences test our resilience, faith, and character. Understanding these challenges as part of the human experience helps us approach them with a mindset geared towards growth and learning.

The Biblical Perspective on Trials

The Bible offers valuable insights into enduring hardships. James 1:2-4, for example, encourages believers to find joy in trials, knowing they produce perseverance. This chapter delves into such scriptures, extracting lessons on how to face challenges with faith and determination.

Developing Resilience

Resilience is the ability to adapt and bounce back from adversity. This chapter discusses key components of resilience, such as a positive attitude, flexibility, and the ability to manage stress effectively. It also covers practical ways to build resilience, including maintaining physical health, cultivating a support network, and developing coping strategies.

Faith as a Source of Strength

In navigating life's challenges, faith can be a significant source of strength. Trusting in God's plan, finding solace in prayer, and leaning on the support of a faith community can provide comfort and guidance during tough times. The chapter highlights how faith can transform our response to adversity, turning obstacles into opportunities for spiritual growth.

Practical Strategies for Navigating Challenges

1. **Problem-Solving:** Developing a systematic approach to tackling challenges.

2. **Emotional Intelligence:** Learning to understand and manage emotions in the face of adversity.

3. **Seeking Wisdom:** Turning to scriptures, mentors, and wise

counsel for guidance and perspective.

4. **Staying Grounded in the Present:** Practicing mindfulness to stay focused and reduce anxiety about the future.

Staying Hopeful in Difficult Times

Maintaining hope is essential in navigating life's challenges. This chapter provides insights into fostering hope, even in the darkest times, through practices like gratitude, visualization of a positive future, and focusing on what can be controlled.

Conclusion

"Navigating Life's Challenges: Strategies for Endurance" is about equipping readers with the tools and insights necessary to face life's challenges head-on. By combining Christian faith with practical resilience strategies, this chapter empowers readers to not only endure hardships but also grow and thrive through them, shaping a reality of strength, perseverance, and hope.

Chapter Ten

The Habit of Happiness: Cultivating Joy Daily

*I*ntroduction

Chapter 9 of "Redefine Your Reality: Shifting Mindsets for Breakthrough Success" delves into the essential pursuit of happiness. Titled "The Habit of Happiness: Cultivating Joy Daily," this chapter explores how happiness is not just an emotion, but a habit that can be cultivated through intentional practices and mindset shifts, underpinned by Christian principles and psychological insights.

Understanding Happiness

Happiness is often perceived as a result of external circumstances. However, this chapter posits that true happiness is a state of being that comes from within. It involves a consistent sense of contentment, joy, and fulfillment, regardless of external situations. We explore the Biblical view of joy, which is often linked to spiritual well-being and a deep-seated peace that transcends circumstances (Philippians 4:4).

The Psychology of Happiness

Psychological research has shown that happiness can be cultivated through specific habits and attitudes. This includes practicing gratitude, nurturing positive relationships, engaging in meaningful activities, and maintaining a healthy balance in life. This chapter integrates these insights with Biblical teachings to offer a holistic approach to developing happiness.

Creating Daily Habits for Happiness

1. **Gratitude:** Incorporating daily practices of gratitude, such as keeping a gratitude journal or sharing thankful thoughts with others.

2. **Mindfulness:** Practicing mindfulness to savor the present moment and appreciate the simple joys of life.

3. **Kindness and Service:** Engaging in acts of kindness and service, as giving to others creates joy and fulfillment.

4. **Positive Affirmations:** Using affirmations to reinforce a positive self-view and outlook on life.

The Role of Faith in Happiness

Faith plays a crucial role in cultivating happiness. Trusting in God's plan, finding contentment in His promises, and engaging in spiritual practices like prayer and worship can significantly contribute to a sense of deep and enduring joy. The chapter discusses how faith can anchor us in happiness, even amidst life's ups and downs.

Overcoming Obstacles to Happiness

While pursuing happiness, we often encounter obstacles such as negative thinking, stress, and external pressures. This chapter offers strategies to overcome these barriers, emphasizing the importance of resilience, a supportive community, and a strong faith foundation.

Conclusion

"The Habit of Happiness: Cultivating Joy Daily" encourages readers to view happiness as a habit that can be developed and nurtured. By integrating practical psychological strategies with Christian teachings, the chapter provides a comprehensive guide for those seeking to infuse their lives with joy, contentment, and a deep sense of fulfillment, irrespective of their external circumstances.

Chapter Eleven

Success Through Service: The Paradox of Giving

*I*ntroduction

In Chapter 10 of "Redefine Your Reality: Shifting Mindsets for Breakthrough Success," we explore a profound paradox at the heart of personal success – the power of giving and service. Titled "Success Through Service: The Paradox of Giving," this chapter delves into how serving others and selflessness can lead to profound personal fulfillment and success, aligning with both Christian values and modern psychological findings.

The Paradox of Giving

The concept that giving can lead to receiving, or that serving others can enhance our own lives, may seem counterintuitive. However, this chapter explores how this paradox is deeply rooted in Christian teachings and backed by psychological research. The act of giving, without the expectation of return, often leads to greater personal and spiritual rewards than the pursuit of self-centered goals.

Service in the Christian Context

In Christianity, service is seen as a fundamental expression of faith and love. Jesus' life and teachings emphasize the importance of serving others as a path to true greatness (Mark 10:45). This chapter examines biblical narratives and teachings that illustrate the transformative power of service and selflessness.

Psychological Benefits of Service

Engaging in acts of service has been shown to have numerous psychological benefits, including increased happiness, reduced stress levels, and a sense of purpose. This chapter discusses these benefits and explains how serving others can lead to a more fulfilling and successful life.

Practical Ways to Serve

1. **Volunteering:** Engaging in community service or volunteering for causes that resonate with your values.

2. **Acts of Kindness:** Incorporating small, everyday acts of kindness into your routine.

3. **Mentorship:** Offering guidance and support to others, sharing your knowledge and experience.

4. **Generosity:** Practicing generosity in various forms, be it through time, resources, or emotional support.

Balancing Service and Self-Care

While service is valuable, it's also essential to balance it with self-care. This chapter offers advice on maintaining this balance, ensuring that the act of giving does not lead to burnout but remains a source of joy and fulfillment.

Conclusion

"Success Through Service: The Paradox of Giving" challenges the conventional understanding of success, highlighting how true fulfillment and achievement are often found in the service of others. By embracing a life of service and generosity, grounded in Christian values and supported by psychological principles, we open ourselves to a deeper, more meaningful form of success.

Chapter Twelve

Overcoming Fear: The Path to Courageous Living

*I*ntroduction

Chapter 11 of "Redefine Your Reality: Shifting Mindsets for Breakthrough Success" focuses on a critical aspect of personal and spiritual growth: overcoming fear. Titled "Overcoming Fear: The Path to Courageous Living," this chapter delves into the nature of fear, its impact on our lives, and practical and spiritual strategies for facing and overcoming it to live a life marked by courage and faith.

Understanding Fear

Fear is a natural human emotion, often rooted in the unknown, uncertainty, or past experiences. While it can serve as a protective mechanism, excessive fear can become a barrier to growth and success.

This chapter explores the psychological and spiritual aspects of fear, including its physical, emotional, and mental manifestations.

The Biblical Perspective on Fear

Scripture offers numerous insights into dealing with fear. Verses like Isaiah 41:10 ("So do not fear, for I am with you; do not be dismayed, for I am your God.") provide comfort and encouragement. This chapter examines such scriptures, showing how faith can be a powerful tool in overcoming fear.

Strategies for Overcoming Fear

This chapter presents both spiritual and practical strategies to conquer fear:

1. **Faith and Trust in God:** Building a strong foundation of faith, trusting in God's protection and guidance.

2. **Understanding and Confronting Fear:** Identifying the root causes of fears and facing them head-on.

3. **Building Resilience:** Developing emotional and mental resilience to handle fears and anxieties.

4. **Positive Affirmations and Prayer:** Using prayer and positive affirmations to reinforce courage and reduce fear.

The Role of Community and Support

Overcoming fear is not a journey to be taken alone. The chapter discusses the importance of a supportive community – family, friends, and faith groups – in providing encouragement, understanding, and support.

Learning from Failures and Setbacks

Fear often arises from the dread of failure or past setbacks. This chapter encourages readers to view failures as opportunities for learning and growth, shifting the perception of fear from a barrier to a stepping stone.

Conclusion

"Overcoming Fear: The Path to Courageous Living" is about transforming the way we perceive and deal with fear. By combining spiritual faith with practical strategies, this chapter guides readers towards a life characterized by courage, resilience, and trust. It's an invitation to step out of the shadows of fear and embrace the light of courageous living.

Chapter Thirteen

Wisdom in Decision Making: Discerning the Best Path

Introduction

Chapter 12 of "Redefine Your Reality: Shifting Mindsets for Breakthrough Success" is dedicated to the art and necessity of wise decision-making. Titled "Wisdom in Decision Making: Discerning the Best Path," this chapter delves into how one can cultivate and apply wisdom in various life decisions, guided by Christian principles and enriched with insights from psychology and practical life experience.

Understanding Wisdom

Wisdom, in both biblical and psychological contexts, is more than knowledge or intelligence. It's the ability to apply knowledge with insight, compassion, and a sense of justice. It involves seeing the bigger picture and considering the long-term consequences and benefits of our actions. This chapter explores the nature of wisdom and its importance in decision-making.

The Biblical Foundation of Wisdom

Scripture is replete with references to wisdom, presenting it as a divine gift and a desirable trait. From Solomon, famed for his wisdom, to the teachings of Jesus, which often focus on wise choices and actions, the Bible offers a rich source of guidance on cultivating wisdom. Key verses and parables that illuminate the concept of wisdom in decision-making are discussed in this chapter.

Practical Steps to Wise Decision-Making

1. **Gathering Information:** Collecting relevant data and insights before making a decision.

2. **Seeking Counsel:** Consulting with trusted advisors, mentors, and scriptural teachings.

3. **Considering Multiple Perspectives:** Looking at decisions from various angles to understand their potential impact.

4. **Prayer and Reflection:** Turning to prayer for divine guidance and clarity in decision-making.

Overcoming Common Decision-Making Pitfalls

The chapter also addresses common pitfalls in decision-making, such as impulsiveness, bias, and overdependence on emotions or logic. It offers strategies to navigate these pitfalls effectively, maintaining a balance between emotional intuition and rational analysis.

The Role of Faith in Decision-Making

Faith plays a pivotal role in wise decision-making. It involves trusting in God's plan and timing, even when the path ahead seems unclear.

This chapter emphasizes how faith, coupled with wisdom, can lead to decisions that are aligned with God's will and beneficial in the long term.

Conclusion

Wisdom in Decision Making: Discerning the Best Path" equips readers with the tools and insights necessary for making wise decisions in various aspects of life. By integrating biblical wisdom, psychological principles, and practical strategies, this chapter guides readers toward thoughtful, informed, and faith-guided decision-making, paving the way for success and fulfillment in their personal and professional lives.

Chapter Fourteen

The Power of Forgiveness: Healing and Reconciliation

Introduction

In Chapter 13 of "Redefine Your Reality: Shifting Mindsets for Breakthrough Success," we explore a deeply transformative aspect of personal and spiritual growth: forgiveness. Entitled "The Power of Forgiveness: Healing and Reconciliation," this chapter delves into the concept of forgiveness, its impact on our lives and relationships, and the role it plays in healing and reconciliation, both from a Christian perspective and a psychological standpoint.

Understanding Forgiveness

Forgiveness is often misunderstood as a sign of weakness or an acceptance of wrongdoing. However, this chapter redefines forgiveness as a powerful act of releasing resentment, anger, and hurt. It is not about condoning harmful actions but about freeing oneself from the burden of negative emotions and moving forward.

Forgiveness in the Bible

The Bible offers profound insights into the nature and importance of forgiveness. From Jesus' teachings on forgiving others "seventy times seven times" (Matthew 18:22) to the parable of the Prodigal Son, scripture highlights forgiveness as a key element of Christian life. This chapter explores these teachings and their practical implications for everyday life.

The Psychological Benefits of Forgiveness

Forgiving others has significant psychological benefits, including reduced stress, improved mental health, and better physical well-being. This chapter examines how forgiveness can lead to emotional healing, enhanced relationships, and personal growth.

Steps to Practicing Forgiveness

1. **Acknowledging Hurt:** Recognizing and accepting the feelings of hurt caused by others.

2. **Empathy:** Trying to understand the perspective and motivations of the person who caused the hurt.

3. **Letting Go:** Actively deciding to release feelings of resentment and bitterness.

4. **Seeking Reconciliation:** Where appropriate, taking steps towards reconciling and rebuilding the relationship.

Forgiving Oneself

In addition to forgiving others, forgiving oneself is crucial for personal peace and growth. This chapter discusses the importance of self-forgiveness, the challenges it involves, and how to practice it effectively.

The Role of Prayer in Forgiveness

Prayer can be a powerful tool in the process of forgiveness. It provides a space for reflection, seeking God's strength and guidance, and aligning our hearts with His grace and mercy. This chapter provides guidance on using prayer to facilitate forgiveness.

Conclusion

"The Power of Forgiveness: Healing and Reconciliation" emphasizes that forgiveness is a choice and a process that can lead to profound healing and freedom. By combining Christian principles with psychological insights, this chapter guides readers towards practicing forgiveness, not only as a moral or spiritual act but as a pathway to personal liberation and enriched relationships.

Chapter Fifteen

Cultivating Gratitude: A Foundation for Abundance

Introduction

Chapter 14 of "Redefine Your Reality: Shifting Mindsets for Breakthrough Success" focuses on a vital but often overlooked aspect of personal growth and fulfillment: gratitude. Titled "Cultivating Gratitude: A Foundation for Abundance," this chapter explores the transformative power of gratitude in shaping a positive outlook on life, enhancing well-being, and attracting abundance, drawing from both Christian teachings and psychological research.

The Essence of Gratitude

Gratitude is more than a feeling of thankfulness in response to receiving benefits; it's a deeper state of appreciation for life itself and the blessings within it, both big and small. This chapter discusses how cultivating a habit of gratitude can change our perception, focusing our attention on abundance rather than lack.

Gratitude in the Bible

The concept of gratitude is deeply rooted in the Bible. Scriptures like 1 Thessalonians 5:18, "give thanks in all circumstances," reflect the Christian ethos of gratitude in every aspect of life. This chapter delves into biblical examples and teachings that emphasize the importance of a grateful heart.

Psychological Benefits of Gratitude

From a psychological perspective, gratitude has been linked to numerous benefits, including increased happiness, reduced depression, and improved relationships. This chapter explores the science behind these benefits, demonstrating how gratitude positively affects our mental and emotional health.

Practices to Cultivate Gratitude

1. **Gratitude Journaling:** Keeping a daily journal to note things for which one is grateful.

2. **Mindful Reflection:** Taking time to reflect on the blessings of life, both in times of prosperity and hardship.

3. **Expressing Gratitude:** Regularly expressing thanks to others, enhancing relationships and spreading positivity.

4. **Gratitude in Prayer:** Incorporating thanksgiving into prayer life, acknowledging God's gifts and provisions.

Overcoming Barriers to Gratitude

Despite its benefits, practicing gratitude can sometimes be challenging, especially in the face of adversity or routine. This chapter discusses common barriers to gratitude, such as negative thinking and taking blessings for granted, offering strategies to overcome these obstacles.

The Role of Gratitude in Attracting Abundance

Gratitude can shift our mindset from scarcity to abundance, opening our hearts and minds to more opportunities and blessings. This chapter examines how a grateful attitude can attract positive experiences and create a cycle of abundance and success.

Conclusion

"Cultivating Gratitude: A Foundation for Abundance" invites readers to embrace gratitude as a daily practice, transforming their outlook on life. By combining scriptural wisdom with practical exercises and psychological insights, this chapter guides readers towards a more grateful, abundant, and fulfilling life.

Chapter Sixteen

Leaving a Legacy: Impacting the World for Good

Introduction

In the final chapter of "Redefine Your Reality: Shifting Mindsets for Breakthrough Success," we focus on the concept of legacy. Titled "Leaving a Legacy: Impacting the World for Good," this chapter explores the importance of creating a lasting, positive impact in the world. It delves into how personal success and fulfillment are intertwined with the contributions we make to others' lives, drawing on Christian teachings and universal principles of philanthropy and service.

Understanding Legacy

Legacy is often associated with wealth and material inheritance, but its true essence lies in the intangible gifts we leave behind: our values, wisdom, and the changes we've inspired in others. This chapter redefines legacy as the footprint we leave on the hearts and lives of people and the world around us.

The Christian Perspective on Legacy

In Christianity, legacy is closely linked to stewardship and service. The Bible encourages believers to use their talents and resources for the greater good. This chapter examines biblical figures who left enduring legacies and draws lessons from their lives about creating lasting impact.

Creating a Personal Legacy

Leaving a legacy begins with living a life of purpose and intention. This chapter provides guidance on identifying personal values and passions and aligning them with actions that positively impact others. It emphasizes the importance of living each day as a contribution to the legacy you wish to leave.

The Role of Service and Philanthropy

Service and philanthropy are key components of a meaningful legacy. This chapter explores various forms of service and giving, encouraging readers to find ways to contribute that resonate with their abilities and passions.

The Impact of Small Actions

Legacy is not only about grand gestures; it's often the small, consistent actions that have the most lasting impact. The chapter highlights how everyday kindness, mentorship, and support can significantly influence others' lives.

Leaving a Spiritual Legacy

For those of faith, leaving a spiritual legacy is paramount. This involves nurturing faith in others, imparting spiritual wisdom, and living a life that reflects Christian principles. The chapter discusses how to integrate faith into the broader concept of legacy.

Conclusion

"Leaving a Legacy: Impacting the World for Good" serves as a cap-stone to the journey of redefining reality. It encourages readers to think beyond personal success to how they can leave a mark on the world. By focusing on service, generosity, and living out one's values, readers are guided towards creating a legacy that not only enriches their lives but also makes a lasting difference in the world.

Chapter Seventeen

Conclusion

Conclusion of "Redefine Your Reality: Shifting Mindsets for Breakthrough Success"

As we conclude our journey through "Redefine Your Reality: Shifting Mindsets for Breakthrough Success," we reflect on the transformative insights and practical wisdom shared across its chapters. This book has been an exploration into the power of mindset, faith, and personal growth, offering a pathway to a life of fulfillment, purpose, and success.

From understanding the power of perspective and embracing the mindset of overcomers, to harnessing the transformative nature of thoughts and the grounding force of faith, each chapter has built upon the last, creating a comprehensive guide for personal and spiritual development. We've delved into the essence of leadership, the strength found in relationships, the peace in prayerful reflection, and the resilience required to navigate life's challenges. We've discovered the joy in cultivating happiness, the fulfillment in service, the courage in overcoming fear, and the discernment in making wise decisions. The power of forgiveness, the richness of gratitude, and the impact of leaving a legacy have rounded out our exploration.

The core message of this book is clear: Redefining your reality is not just about changing your circumstances but about transforming your mindset, aligning your actions with your deepest values, and living a life rooted in faith and purpose. It's about seeing beyond the surface of your experiences to the deeper spiritual truths that guide them.

As readers move forward, they are equipped not only with knowledge but also with the tools to apply these principles in their daily lives. The journey of personal transformation is ongoing, and "Redefine Your Reality" serves as a companion and guide for this journey. The book encourages continuous growth, learning, and the pursuit of a life that not only seeks personal success but also contributes positively to the lives of others.

In closing, "Redefine Your Reality: Shifting Mindsets for Breakthrough Success" is more than just a book; it's a call to action. It's an invitation to step into a fuller, more meaningful existence, to embrace the challenges and joys of life with a renewed perspective, and to make a lasting impact on the world. The journey of transformation awaits, and the power to redefine your reality lies within you.

About the Author

"I was born as the answer to the Cry of Many."

Cyprian Ahuchaogu is more than a life coach and a minister of the gospel; he is a beacon of hope and wisdom, guiding many towards a path of enlightenment and spiritual fulfillment. As a renowned author, his bibliography is a testament to his commitment to spreading knowledge and inspiration. His works, including titles like "Thoughts of Treasure," "Thoughts of Treasure Digest," "The Power of God's Word," "The Power of Love," "The Battlefield of the Soul," "Prayer Made Simple: Praying the Scriptures, the Word and His Will 365 Days," "The Job Seeker's Bible: A Step-by-Step Guide to Updating Your Resume and Landing Your Dream Job," and "Just Get Started: The Complete Guide to Writing High-Quality Assignments, Essays,

Dissertations, and Theses With Ease and Grade High," have touched the lives of many.

Cyprian's writing is a unique blend of insightful and thought-provoking perspectives on faith and mindset. Each book he crafts is not just a piece of writing but a journey into deeper understanding, connection to Christ, and personal transformation. His goal is to expand minds to new possibilities and foster spiritual growth and development, challenging readers to critically think and realize their potential within the embrace of Christ.

Beyond the written word, Cyprian's eloquence and wisdom resonate through his speaking engagements. He is a gifted orator, known for captivating and empowering his audience with messages that encourage them to strive for greatness and embrace the principles of the kingdom.

His presence extends into the digital world, where he connects with a global audience. On platforms like Facebook (Cyprian Chiabughiotu Ahuchaogu), TikTok (Cyprian J Ahuchaogu), YouTube (Success Mentorship with Cyprian), and Twitter (Cyprian Ahuchaogu), he shares insights and motivational content, furthering his mission to inspire and guide individuals on their spiritual and personal development journey.

Cyprian Ahuchaogu's life and work are dedicated to lighting a path for others. Through his writing, speaking, and online presence, he continues to motivate, energize, and guide individuals in their pursuit of greatness, anchored in the profound truths of the Christian faith.

Also By

Afterword

Afterword

As we close the final pages of "Redefine Your Reality: Shifting Mindsets for Breakthrough Success," I hope you find yourself not at the end of a journey, but standing at the threshold of a new beginning. This book was written with the intention of guiding, inspiring, and empowering you to embark on a path of personal transformation and success.

Throughout the chapters, we navigated the complex terrains of mindset shift, faith, leadership, relationships, and legacy. Each section was designed not only to provide insights and knowledge but also to encourage introspection and application in your daily life. The goal was never just to inform but to transform.

If there is one core message to take away from this book, it is that you have the power to redefine your reality. The tools, strategies, and principles outlined in these pages are meant to serve as your compass, helping you to navigate the challenges and opportunities that life presents.

As you move forward, I encourage you to revisit these chapters whenever you need guidance or inspiration. Transformation is an ongoing process, and this book can continue to be a resource as you grow and evolve.

I would also like to extend my heartfelt gratitude to you, the reader, for embarking on this journey with me. Your willingness to explore new ideas and embrace change is a testament to your commitment to personal growth and success.

Finally, I hope that the messages within this book resonate with you, not just in your mind but in your heart and spirit. May they inspire you to live a life that is aligned with your highest values and aspirations, a life that not only seeks personal success but also contributes positively to the lives of others.

Thank you for sharing this journey with me. May you continue to grow, thrive, and redefine your reality in ways that bring you joy, fulfillment, and success.

Blessings and best wishes,

Cyprian Ahuchaogu

Acknowledgements

Acknowledgments

The journey of writing "Redefine Your Reality: Shifting Mindsets for Breakthrough Success" has been as transformative for me as I hope it will be for you, the reader. This book, a mosaic of ideas, experiences, and lessons, would not have been possible without the support, guidance, and inspiration from a number of remarkable individuals.

First and foremost, I extend my deepest gratitude to God, whose unwavering love and wisdom have been my guiding light throughout this journey. It is in His strength that I have found the courage to pursue this endeavor and in His grace that I have seen it to fruition.

I am profoundly thankful to my family, whose love and support have been my constant source of strength. To my spouse and children, for their patience and encouragement, and to my parents and siblings, for their endless belief in my vision and purpose.

My heartfelt appreciation goes to my mentors and spiritual leaders, who have imparted invaluable wisdom and guidance. Your insights and teachings have not only shaped my personal journey but have also deeply influenced the contents of this book.

A special thanks to my editorial team, whose expertise and dedication have been instrumental in bringing this manuscript to life. Your attention to detail, commitment to excellence, and creative input have been invaluable.

I am also grateful to my peers and colleagues, who provided feedback, encouragement, and constructive criticism. Your perspectives and experiences have enriched this work in countless ways.

To the many friends, community members, and readers who have shared their stories and insights with me, thank you. Your experiences and struggles have been a significant source of inspiration and have added depth and authenticity to this book.

Lastly, I extend my appreciation to you, the reader, for embarking on this journey with me. Your willingness to explore new ideas and commit to personal growth is what ultimately gives this book its purpose and meaning.

Thank you all for being a part of this journey. May we continue to grow, learn, and redefine our realities for the better.

With gratitude,

Cyprian Ahuchaogu